Field Kno

D1256719

Field Knowledge

Morri Creech

Foreword by

J. D. McClatchy

WAYWISER

First published in 2006 by

THE WAYWISER PRESS

9 Woodstock Road, London N4 3ET, UK
P.O. Box 6205, Baltimore, MD 21206, USA
www.waywiser-press.com

Managing Editor
Philip Hoy

Associate Editors
Joseph Harrison   Clive Watkins   Greg Williamson

A CIP catalogue record for this book is available from the British Library

ISBN-10: 1-904130-23-2   ISBN-13: 978-1-904130-23-9

Library of Congress Cataloging-in-Publication Data

Creech, Morri, 1970-
  Field knowledge / Morri Creech ; foreword by J. D. McClatchy.
    p. cm.
  Poems.
  ISBN-13: 978-1-904130-23-9
  I. McClatchy, J. D., 1945- II. Title.
  PS3603.R44F54 2006
  811'.6--dc22

                                        2006020874

Printed and bound by
Cromwell Press Ltd., Trowbridge, Wiltshire

for Hattie

Acknowledgements

Thanks to the editors of the following journals, who have published a number of poems from this collection: *Critical Quarterly* (U.K.), *The Hudson Review, The New Criterion, The New Republic, Sewanee Review, Southeast Review, The Southern Review, Tar River Poetry, 21st: The Journal of Contemporary Photography, Verse Daily.*

"Engine Work: Variations" originally appeared in *Paper Cathedrals* (Kent State University Press, 2001).

Many of the poems were originally published in *The Book of Life* and *Listening to the Earth,* two limited, signed editions created in collaboration with the art photographer Robert ParkeHarrison and published by *21st.*

Contents

Foreword by J. D. McClatchy

There are austere poets whose very distance from the world and whose reticent style create a tension that brings the experience described and the poem enacted into a sharper, more heartbreaking focus. And there are luxuriant poets – poets like Keats and Whitman and Hopkins – for whom the world's bounty and the heart's bottomless mysteries spill over into lines that almost burst with excess. Morri Creech is a luxuriant, but a canny one. He knows that the very grounds for his celebrations – abundance and appetite – are deceptive. The world's alluring detail, and the Faustian impulse to stay the moment, can distract from impending dangers: disillusion, despair, mortality.

> So once a man lost sight,
> near Pompeii, of history's beginnings,
> caught in some lavish *now*
>
> of appetite – the flush of sex, the steam
> rising from his bathwater –
> in all that languor failing to note the wind
> stir the trickled streams
> along his flanks, the mountain sound its thunder,
> or those first warm snows descend.

Creech's attention to the drama of extravagance is not merely a physical one – though it is difficult for me to think of a contemporary poet with a more exact eye and lavish lexicon. When he looks out, he also sees the world beneath the world, and realizes "the place is gone / where the heart would know its object, and be known." A sensual fullness, in other words, matched by an emotional wholeness. There is, in these poems, an ache for what the poet wants to believe existed in more than his own mind. The world "repeats but cannot mend" the rift between our lives and our imaginings. If our lives now lack the consequence afforded by myth, we remain haunted by the possibility: "It wasn't the god we missed, / but how a god might sound." We are stranded "among the disenchantments of our longing." Still, this poet's sad music gives a lyric intensity to the irony. Among his sweet gum groves and feed stores, the white-washed fences and simmering violence, he is our Southern Orpheus, and his plangent lines rise to every occasion:

> More than the sounds that set the stones and trees
> in place, and that arrange both shade and light,
> a sad music ripens in the heart; caught
> between oblivion and paradise,
> it enters the world as loss, though in such ways
> that the cadences of grief resound as praise.

When writing of the self – for a century now it has seemed the only available subject – many poets like to flash the cracked glass slide of private memory onto the page's screen. Creech prefers more amplitude, and draws on a range of classical and biblical allusions, on the choreography of rhetoric, on the complexities of science and nature. He can work up a trope – as when the rebel angels cheat in heaven's casino or Orpheus is portrayed as an aging rock star – with a witty virtuosity, and can soar to dizzying heights of sublimity. At one point he compares his assembling of poems to his grandfather tinkering with car engines, and in fact his stanzaic schemes are precision-built, oiled and gleaming.

Robert Frost once remarked that if a book has twenty-five poems in it, the book itself is the twenty-sixth. Creech begins his book in his grandfather's backyard, and ends it in his own. Between the span of generations, in the very middle of the book, the long title poem is a touching anatomy of rural history and memory. Braced by family and region, then, the poems in either flank of the book summon variations on a few recurring themes and figures, though the tone of the book clearly darkens as more material is gathered into its meditation.

For all his technical skill, in each individual poem and in the conversation among them, Morri Creech remains a rhapsodist at heart, and he has made a book in which a reader can both lose and find himself. *Field Knowledge* is a rare achievement, and a lasting one.

... whose zero in His winter's mercy
Still hides the undecipherable seed.

– Howard Nemerov

Engine Work: Variations

June morning. Sunlight flashes through the pines.
Blue jays razz and bicker, perch on a fence post
back of my grandfather's yard. His stripped engines
clutter the lawn. And everywhere the taste
of scuppernongs just moments off the vines,
so sour that you would swear the mind has traced
a pathway through the thicket, swear the past
comes clear again, picked piecemeal from the dust – .

⁂

Or else it's late – September – and the shade
thicker than I recall: those cardinals,
finches or mockingbirds still haven't made
a sound all afternoon, though ripe fruit swells
on vine, or branch – or bramble. Thus the frayed
edge of recollection slowly ravels
away to nothing, until that place is gone
where the heart would know its object, and be known.

⁂

All right. Not to begin with those backlit pines,
those scuppernongs, the jay perched on a branch
of sweet gum – no, oak, I think. With what, then?
With my grandfather holding a torque wrench
or ratchet? Some old engine's stammer and whine
before it starts, or doesn't – a house finch,
singing or silent? Language, too, seems wrong,
though it's all I have. *Grandfather. Scuppernong.*

⁂

To fix him in some moment, word for word,
that man who taught me gears and cylinders, sweat,
precision of machinery – the hard

love of assembling things.
                              I know the heat
all summer hung like a scrim where pistons fired
and the boy I was watched in the raw sunlight.
Spilled oil rainbowed in its shallow pan.
One bird call, maybe; fruit on a trellised vine ...

Impossible not to change things, move the words
from here to there. It's late now. Nothing's settled –
not engine noise or the sound of one far bird
the mind sings true. Which version of the world
should I believe? This morning in the yard
scuppernongs hang and sweeten. Pine boughs yield
some fragment of the blue jay's call, a sound
the resonant air repeats but cannot mend.

World Enough

Swift as a weaver's shuttle, time unspools
     its hours in glistening threads
and rapturous polychromes – in the arc of leaf
     or feather toward the pools
of that deep shade to which the morning weds
     its brilliance, in a brief

slur of redwings above the white-washed fence,
     the sprinkler's lisp and hiss
trailing a veil of diamond through the air –
     and spins a present tense
of such dizzying concords one is apt to miss
     much of the affair.

Think of those vast histories that have gone
     unnoticed or unseen:
ants marching on some martial expedition,
     defending their Babylon
of mounds and chambered catacombs between
     the posts of the Crucifixion,

bees building their honey in the walls
     at Jericho or Troy –
whole catalogs of kingdoms and empires,
     straw-built citadels,
Spenglerian cycles of health and slow decay,
     all lost in the spangled fires

of daylight, the rich flux of hours and years.
     Amid such dense detail
it's easy to miss the moment when Atropos
     bends close with her shears
to cut the taut threads, until their tensions fail
     and time's grip turns loose;

easy, in Eden's commerce of sunlight,
    wild fruit and stippled wings,
to miss the cormorant bristling on the bough.
    So once a man lost sight,
near Pompeii, of history's beginnings,
    caught in some lavish *now*

of appetite – the flush of sex, the steam
    rising from his bathwater –
in all that languor failing to note the wind
    stir the trickled streams
along his flanks, the mountain sound its thunder,
    or those first warm snows descend.

The Canto of Ulysses

Primo Levi, in his apartment in Turin, reading *The Divine Comedy*. February, 1987

Drowsing, head propped above the eighth circle,
he feels the present shifting like a keel,
takes his bearings by the toss and swivel

of snow in window light – though still less real,
it seems to him, than that thick Polish snow
which, tumbling in his mind, begins to wheel

like Dante's leaves or starlings, like the slow
stumble of shades from an open freight car,
or from an open book. All night, the snow

whirls at his window, whiting out the stars.
We sailed now for the stars of that other pole.
Leafing a thumb-worn page, he tries to parse

those lines he once struggled to recall
for a fellow prisoner, who'd hoped to learn
Italian as they scraped rust from the wall

of an emptied petrol tank. *The greater horn
began to mutter and move, as a wavering flame
wrestles against the wind and is overworn –*

although, oddly enough, the lines sound tame
now there is no one to explain them to.
Nor words to write. His own canticle of pain

is, after all, finished. The past is nothing new.
And the present breaks over him like the dream
of firelight, plush eiderdown, and hot stew

a prisoner will sometimes startle from
who has lost hope of returning to the world,
blowing upon his hands the pluming steam

of breath, in which a few snowflakes are whirled.
Or, nodding above the passage where Ulysses
tells how the second journey ended – hurled

by a *fierce squall,* till *the sea closed over us* –
he feels at the moment like that restless king
home from Troy after twenty years, his face

grown old and strange from so much wandering,
who broods all night over the cyclops' lair
or Circe's pigs, the shades' dim gathering,

then falls asleep.
           He leans back in his chair.
It all seems now just like it seemed – the snow;
the frozen dead. They whisper on the stair

as if he'd called their shades up from below
to hear the story of Agamemnon slain,
or paced out the long maze of the *Inferno*

to hear their lamentations fresh again.
Beyond his window: stars, the sleeping town,
the past, whirled like flakes on a windowpane –

the sea closed over us, and the prow went down.
Dreaming, he drops the book without a sound.

Last Days of Orpheus

As for the songs, he still remembered them –
that, at least, was nice; and down the hall
the peevish landlord on his rounds was known
to hum with real feeling. But the days seemed small

and untuned now. He sulked or slept, an old man
in a rented room whose face no one recalled
from record sleeves or posters of the band;
who kept to himself, thick-waisted, a little bald.

There remained, nevertheless, the minor harmonies
of sun and leaf, some clouds and half a moon
to charm the dull hours; or, at times, a phrase
from Brahms or Mahler on the gramophone –

but trees his song swept had resumed their stations;
the wind, stunned to a doldrum by his voice,
now wore at the same gray stone. The audience
of shades had long ago turned toward the noise

and boredom to which the dead are so accustomed.
What was he left with? – photographs, a sheet
or two of notes on which a snowing dust
settled, a bride's gown hung neatly in the closet.

And little else that proved to him the past
was real, or mattered much. He could believe,
for instance, that he sang once in the mist,
the big venues of Hell: here were the sheaves

where he had scrawled the music. He felt sure
someone had listened, sure a fallen leaf
rose to its branch in sympathy: the measures,
repeating in his mind, composed his grief.

He closed his eyes. Perhaps it had been real –
the grandeurs of the stage; love. Yet the years
looked to him like the bride caught in a spell
who winks, then turns her back and disappears.

No matter that he could not retrieve them now.
He remembered a girl's face, her wedding ring
flashing, remembered a place of grief and shadow.
And, as he remembered, he began to sing.

Some Notes on Grace and Gravity

1. Giotto

The postured myths of Byzantines? Ho-hum.
Leave Cimabue the manner and the gaze
of saints whose sandals never bore their weight,
their very gowns stunned to beatitude –
but if two men kiss at Gethsemane
there should be torchlight and the crush of mobs,
a keen blade raised to glance the soldier's ear.
Let there be lutes and fiddles to attend
the virgin's marriage; or, say, at the gate
where Anna and Joachim may sometime meet,
the common stir and gossiping of girls.
Saints in their figured scenes shall stand before
the fur of shepherds' boots, the dogs and sheep,
and there shall be much fidgeting of gowns
amid the old hosannas, the actual heft
and weight of angel wings to brush the ground.

2. Leonardo

Christ at the table, Mary among the rocks.
A grace, he knew, lay hidden in their limbs
that lay, too, in the limbs of criminals,
the twist and torque of carpenters' bare shoulders,
even the faces of his ugly children –
when asked why his own offspring looked so poor
compared to the rich productions of his brush,
he'd once replied, "I make paintings by day,
children at night." And it had been at night
in a church basement, one old story goes,
that the artist set aside his brush and palette,
lifted a surgeon's knife above the table,
and found the grace of hangmen and of saints
lay not in the spirit's quickenings and motion,
but stretched out in the sinews' long striations,
in webbed integument and the curve of bone.

3. Newton

A minor disappointment not to find
angels pushing the planets around their courses
as Leibnitz believed. A shame, but not a great one,
that the universe seemed less and less to hang
glimmering from God's chain like a golden fob,
although a pendent weight shaped Newton's thought.

Sitting alone there in that storied orchard,
he'd seen the apples drooping from their boughs;
until one formed, unplucked, a grand conclusion.
The apple fell because it had to fall,
as objects move toward objects, in accord.
It struck a dizzying tune into his head.

The clockwork of the heavens may make music,
but it was a grave music that he heard,
the whirl of mass, the hum of centrifuge,
and calculations on the page would prove
such motion both a falling and a flight.
Thus bodies spin each other round in space.

And gravity, too, becomes a kind of grace.

For the Rebel Angels

Heaven is a casino. Bright. No clocks.
Everyone strikes it rich on the rigged machines.

But a few would like to find out what it means
to come up short, crap out, to take hard knocks.

They've known too long the splendor of Pure Being.
The booze they drink has no effect at all.

But some would like to stumble drunk, to fall
down on a cocktail girl and grab her wings.

They whisper out of earshot of the pit boss.
Each one shuffles a deck tucked in his feathers.

They're talking odds, they're shrugging off the tethers
of a sure thing, they're weighing risk and loss.

The rakish haloes slump in the swank light.
They shed a few bronze quills and make their way.

Now each of them sleeves a card and starts to play.
With luck, they may lose everything tonight.

The Resurrection of the Body

for Keith Carter

Not quite, I think, what the pious would have prayed for,
these bodies flayed and hived to such permanence –
but you should know that in Florence, down a long corridor
smelling of beeswax, formaldehyde, and dust, a room opens
onto the afterlife. Past skulls arranged and numbered
in the pristine chambers of the ossuary, past jarred infants
pickled in suspension, dwarf limbs brined and labeled word for word
in that dead language sacred to God and science,
you are permitted at last to enter upon that hall
alone, without a guide, to commit the casual sacrilege
of looking. You should keep silent there among the cells,
the treasuries of glass catacombs, if you would gauge
their mysteries, would make out the faintly audible hum
like an angel's labored breath, the stir of seraphic wings
pressing against the stone door of a tomb
not emptied but transfigured, or like the murmurings
of bees, a sound that is merely the current's
dull surge through fluorescent lights blazing overhead
and gusts of cold air from the hundred vents
that preserve and tend the chambers of the dead.

Down that hall which opens on such depths of understanding
as memory cannot plumb within the soul,
twinned heads, their occipitals fused together, hang
Janus-faced above fleams and styptics, forceps and bone chisels,
and the corpse whose legs are swollen to balloons
stands propped beside a text of scriptured flesh, the flesh made word
in a long series of two-inch thick incisions –
cleaned, cross-sectioned and neatly drained of blood,
then wedged between panes of the clearest glass,
pages in which are pressed the layered revelations
of sinew and ligament, lymph nodes, lungs and pancreas,
the nerves' branchwork, down to the knotted rosary of spine;

but if you keep moving, careful not to loiter among the viscid
relics, vanities of those who hoped the intellect
could reach the end of that unending road,
if you look ahead, your attention fixed
on distant archways and ever-opening chambers,
you will reach a place where every light is muted,
dimmed on these wax revenants writhing in postures
of breached ecstasy. Each figure here was resurrected
from hundreds of dissections, hundreds of anonymous
subjects who believed the body is immortal,
would be raised again from the corpse-seed, the dross
of blood and marrow, not from the emptied cells
of honey bees, their combs melted to fill
plaster molds of exposed viscera,
then shaped to the martyred gestures of these models
gazing back from the dust of a different era –

think of Bartholomew prone beneath the blade,
saints so wedded to their pain
the reward for unerring faith seems paid
with each sweep of the knife, the shrill refrain
of metal scoring bone; or conquered Marsyas,
body drawn from its sheath, peeled from the swaddling-bands
that death unwinds. One form still displays
its cut and raveled skin draped from an outstretched hand,
the other hand clutching the bloodied knife.
A woman extends full length on her divan,
arm thrown back in the languor of spent desire, true to life
except for the skull uncorked to expose the brain,
the dermal mask bisected, so that if you leaned close
enough, you could reach your hand inside
the wound, trace each branch along the lymphatic pathways,
could believe the furrowed bone, the blood's halt tide,

but you should take care. Though this is a medical museum,
where every niche and chamber is consecrated
to certainties – each looped intestine, each limb
and cancered torso indexed, catalogued, and dated –
though cell to synapse we know the woof and texture
of human tissue, science will not explain
the swarm of immensities raging there
beyond the precincts of lens or lancet, explain
this ravaged flesh redeemed in wax
twisted to the postures of the living, nor account for why
centuries after the bone saws and scalpels extracted
the tender briskets, their forms compel the eye –
science does not account for why our gaze
lingers on the flayed resurrections of another age
long after the mind has gleaned from their hived bodies
the honey of knowledge.

In the Orchards of Science

for Dafydd Wood

If knowledge increases unreality, then
what have we got here? These aren't the orchards
Berkeley might have dreamt up, some mirage
of conceptual fruit, fugitive as words –
leaves, branches, and ripe apples all as thought-born
as the goddess sprung from Zeus's mind and rage.

Nor quite those orchards where, the legend tells us,
Newton felt nature's grave principles compel
an apple loosened from its bough to drop,
pummeling him toward thoughts that would dispel
centuries of error, when with his calculus
he'd conjure a God whose heavens could not stop.

Here nothing's certain, though the fruit is real:
as fixed in its pendent tensions, in its mass
and groundward proclivities as any fruit
our hands have picked before, of course; no less
sleek to the touch, no less accountable
to time – its luster, too, is beyond dispute –

except that one may perceive the void heart
of matter seething from a core laid bare
in quantum calculations, in abstruse
theorems beyond what the eye or hand can chart:
the frenzied spin of electrons, the stir
of still apples on their solid, windless boughs.

And may perceive, as Oppenheimer once,
a strange deity ripening in that fruit:
no sustainer clutching in his hand the whorled
conch of creation, but in the flash of light
blazing from a breached cluster of nucleons
the radiant god, shatterer of worlds.

Regarding the Windmaker

Job speaks in old age
Wilt thou break a leaf driven to and fro? and wilt thou pursue the dry stubble?

The voice from the whirlwind hushed,
having gotten the last word –
it's His right, I suppose.
But no word from the Lord

has stirred the dust of these hills
for a long time. Sure, the skein
of the wind still unravels,
calling to mind again

that day the joists and stanchions
gave, and the house collapsed
on my first, cherished sons;
that day the Lord's gifts lapsed,

my fever rose, and boils
scourged my flesh. And the clouds,
of course, still hang balanced
above the fields, to shroud

their architect's intentions.
What good would it have done
to complain, fenced as I am
with ligament and bone?

Each night my wife would touch
the sprawling constellations
of scars across my back –
more numerous than the nations

once promised to Abraham.
And dreams of those first children
Jehovah has since replaced
would remind me of some sin,

some broken law I couldn't
quite put my finger on –
until, come morning, I'd hear
the clamor of that spawn

the Lord has blessed me with
gathering round my bed;
oh, I've kept faith with Him,
it hardly needs be said.

For the man who has no faith
in God, *his* hopes shall ebb
and slacken; and his trust
shall be a spider's web.

But when that wind has shaken
the fine-spun filaments
of the just man's sweat and labor,
and when that man repents

for crimes he cannot name,
who then will give account?
For years I slept uneasy,
felt my suspicions mount.

One night I dreamt an angel
spoke, and as his radiance
spilled out across my floor,
things started to make sense:

"Hail Job, the butt and brunt
of the great celestial prank!
As for your cosmic pratfall,
it's me you've got to thank;

the Lord, too, played his part.
For years His nostrils gloried
in your pious sacrifice,
and He kept faith in your storied

righteousness; all it took
was a few well-chosen words
before His doubts set in,
and soon you saw your herds

and all your servants razed
to ash beneath His fire:
a thunderous laughter rose
from the seraphic choir.

You've got your compensation
just the same. Sleep well now, Job.
But know whose steps you hear
treading across the globe."

And waking, I remembered
those days I spoke my peace –
pointless, really. I keep quiet
now, living out my lease

among that brood of children,
my consolation prize;
and keep myself indoors
when the wind begins to rise,

until He lays me down
and the Lord spreads His shade,
who could not keep covenant
with what His hands have made.

Colloquy at Salt Point

Fine, of course, to believe
the end is gold-stitched gowns and garish light,
that the long patience of loam and roots will sieve
us clean till some sheer element takes flight,

harping above the roofs
its high-toned ditty. But down-strand from the bay
landscape yields only the harsher proofs –
the tide's simmer, the old broth of decay

rendering back to muck
whatever washes here: whelk or feather star,
a tern's wing sprawled out in the drawl and suck
of mud, rank oils, and brine. Near the sand bar

three herring gulls attend
the dead skate wedged beneath a busted keel.
In a seethe of marsh and cordgrass, the salt wind
tumbles a carapace.
                        It's just as well

if here no trumpets raise
the triggerfish up from its scattered bones,
the one-eyed mullet from the crab that flays
it down to raw matter, flenses and hones

gill, fin, and freckled scale
to an absence clean and absolute as noon light.
What better hymn than the gnats' faint canticle
for these, caught in the round of appetite

that feasts on what it feeds?
Honey of generation, the compost's reek –
it's all the same to bluebottles that breed
in a lamprey's carcass, to the poor and meek

festering in the sedge.
Here, where first worlds and the next converge
in sump and spawnings at the inlet's edge,
if our own lives finally emptied to the surge

of a tide's rich swill,
could it be praise enough that the crayfish brings
its hunger, that the oyster builds its shell
amid the brineflies' shimmer, a haze of wings?

Listening to the Earth

after the photograph by Robert ParkeHarrison

We'd heard the prophets speak,
knew well their eloquent thunder, the split stone
and urgent whirlwind of their voice and word,
had grown used to the fierce synaptic streaks
of flame, the olive-bearing birds
and withered fields that figured their concern.

But what we'd never heard
was their silence: the wind grown inarticulate
at their retreat from us, the god's command
hushed in the trees – a voice they'd said had stirred
for our ears that we might understand
what now, plainly, none of us could interpret.

At first we were relieved;
such talk of mystery and consequence
when there was work to do, laundry and errands,
the grain waiting for harvest. So we lived
unhindered for a while, our minds
less cluttered, clearer, fixed in the present tense.

But who would read the hail,
storms and stars, the pale fever of winter sun
or those first harsh winds that flushed the moon's gold,
swept the corn and mellowed the plums each fall?
Who was there to say what the world
meant? The raven's flight, bees sweetening carrion,

had little to do with us;
the sparrow's note was foreign to our ears.
Breezes stirred in the eaves much as before,
it seemed, but kept on saying less and less
about us. On the granary floor
the scattered chaff would not speak to our fears.

It wasn't the god we missed,
but how a god might sound, those metaphors
and tropes that yoked us to some vast design,
threshing hidden shades up out of the mist,
or lilies that neither toil nor spin,
beneath a sky now strewn with random stars.

And in the plain streets we listened
for those syllables that once conjured the cold,
fathomless swells of Leviathan-haunted seas,
the fabled bush ablaze on hallowed ground,
and snowflakes' mythic treasuries
transfiguring our ordinary fields.

Windwriting

Autumn has coaxed the cold leaves into flame.
Sun motes tumble, then settle on your sill.
The wind is writing down a few more names.

You lean your head against the window frame,
Watching the steam rise from the sewer grill.
Autumn has coaxed the cold leaves into flame

Where children on the sidewalk play their games
Of Hide and Seek, You're It, as children will.
The wind is writing down a few more names –

Something to do, perhaps, with an old shame,
Some nasty thing that Jack once did to Jill?
Autumn has coaxed the cold leaves into flame,

And soon the hour will go the way it came.
Trees, like Birnam Wood, crowd toward the hill.
The wind is writing down a few more names;

Though not yours, surely. How are you to blame?
Your papers are in order. You've paid your bills.
Still autumn coaxes the cold leaves into flame.
The wind keeps writing, writing down the names.

Firstfruits

But now is Christ risen from the dead,
and become the firstfruits of them that slept.
– Corinthians 15:20

You've heard it before, I'm sure,
how the vault of heaven will strew its vital gold
a thousand pieces, bright as an angel's gown
    in the sweet, consummate hour
when all that the saints and prophets have foretold
comes true: the dead raised up, each mortal coil
    wound firm on the spindled bone,
and love at last unbounded by despair
    or the grave confines of soil.

    Rumors have often bred
in choir lofts, barber shops, on the front steps
of the local five and dime – how Pee Wee Gaskins,
    now locked in his cell, was said
to have killed at least a hundred, how the tulips
on the church lawn one morning were seen to blaze
    gold with the lucent skins
of five copperheads: till everyone agreed
    these were the final days.

    Or so it seemed that summer
When floodtides razed the coast. You've read, of course,
that flesh is bare grain, like unto a seed,
    that no one knows the hour
of the Lord's design – but storm winds gathered force,
blasting the rain against the window glass,
    steeping the lawns to mud,
and even those of us who lived this far
    inland could hear the toss

    and whiplash of tall pines,
steeples plucked from churches, the hiss of downed wire.
Still, who could have predicted what we'd wake to?

Not even Pee Wee Gaskins
brooding over his strangled girls could conjure
what lay in the light that gilded one soaked field,
    lay strewn beneath a rainbow
spanning the far pasture when the last rains
    hushed. It was not the world

    we hoped for. There they were,
the dead returned as we had never known them
in life, some kneeling against a fallen tree
    or face down in the water,
washed from the graves to constitute their kingdom;
and, sun-touched near the pasture's edge – *O Death*
    where is thy victory,
thy sting? – an infant swaddled in coils of fence wire,
    snagged on a harrow's teeth.

Suspension

From just such stillness, once, the world was made.
        A few clouds hang suspended,
moored to their pale reflections on the sea,
        and cast as pure a shade
on stone and windless tide as before time ended
        the lull of eternity.

No driftwood lies brined or broken on the sand;
        terns have yet to glean
from the reeds some fish or shattered carapace.
        For miles along the strand
water hems the shoreline, hushed and pristine
        as on a painter's canvas.

A sourceless light finds out each least detail:
        the jeweled transparencies
of scales and silicates, a tide pool's mezzotint,
        the bright edges of shale
we know will disappear when by degrees
        the tide draws back, is spent

against the rocks, and the narrative unfolds.
        Arnold, of course, looked out
on such a calm, though he'd soon hear the clash
        and grating roar, behold
Thucydides' armies and the surge of doubt,
        his whole life awash;

God, too, looked once, and thought the finished work
        good, before the hour
began its swift concatenation and brought
        by chance or choice the quirk
that spoiled His paradise, the fruit turned sour
        when man awoke to thought –

Suspension

Who can say what this stillness might portend?
      Impossible to know;
though soon some drift of wings may seem to us
      raven or dove, the wind
recall the Lord's first breath or come to sow
      the seed of a darker promise.

Dream of the Burning

It was snow I had wanted as a child
in the fever of summer,
clean white flakes to ease the August heat.
All night, while threads of smoke
raveled from the barn's mended rooftop,
while my father, stripped to the waist,
dug trenches to keep the flames
from the boards of our house,
I slept undisturbed at my cousin's
and dreamt a fine powder
settled into locust branches,
window screens, the furrows of my palms.
The next morning I stood
ankle deep in the reeking cinder
of barn wood, horse flesh, fence timber –
all that lay buried in the wreckage –
to sift the remains
for something salvageable.
On the porch, my mother wept into her hands,
not wanting to believe
how things go up
in the lulling monotony of weather
to expose a layer of sod
black as hearth stone.

My father reached into the charred loam,
hauled out a hayrake,
a horse's femur,
and the dream whirled
like smoke in the silence between us.
Ash feathered his shoulders,
covered the field, the scorched brush
he would scour all morning
for evidence: tipped lantern,
lightning-kissed oak trunk,
box of kitchen matches

pitched into the brambles.
For hours I hid beneath the smoldering
trellis of muscadines, praying,
it's not my fault, Jesus I didn't do it,
so long I began to doubt
my own innocence. And as I squinted
through the veil of settling dust,
I imagined the light
splintering down
between me and my father,
spreading along the shattered length
of the barn, the tobacco field,
everything ablaze and unforgiving.

Elegy of False Accord

Who hasn't heard the story – Orpheus
and his famous measures, the rush of notes that made
rivers change their courses, stones and trees
tune themselves to his lyre and matchless voice,
the whole world rearranged to fit a song?

Who wouldn't want to believe such cadences –
believe that the sun pulled back the scrim of shade,
and wind, enchanted by those melodies,
lay hushed in the autumn leaves which ceased to fall
at least for a little while, at least as long
as Orpheus kept playing?

                      But trace the skein
of all that lovely singing to its source,
back through the swept hair of willow and cypress,
beyond mute chambers and the lightless halls
of Hades, the backward look and its remorse –

a bride lies still and bitten in a wood
long before that first thorned note begins.
Unwind the skein, it all leads back to this:

the hour, the grief, the poison in the blood.

Field Knowledge

for Kevin Meaux

Kitfield, S. C.

As if time were a pearl of great price still treasured up here
among snags of sumac, dockweed and the froth of honeysuckle,
fallows so cluttered with scrub pine a back hoe would slip its gear,

as if you could prize from weeds and loam one immaculate
hour, one orient pearl buried at the damp root, and lift it clear
of the years of corn stalks, furrows, hay rakes freckled with scat – .

It was late summer in the year. Wind worried the pine limbs,
shifted the scattered grain in the clawfoot tub where the horses ate.
There was no following the sound of that wind back to the hymns

the Huguenot fathers sang here. No stone or fence rail
marked where the chapel was that men stripped to the bare frames
nor marked where the plundered brick foundation lay, the bell

hauled off, stolen or bartered, and melted for pig iron in 1864,
the quoins and brass fixtures ferried upriver for quick sale,
all the old bricks new-laid for the grade school and general store.

To find that place again you'd need more than the cicada's shell
jeweling the oak, the daubers' mortared nest, need more
than the slurred scripture the snake traces on the floor of the stable.

You'd have to pray and wait like a prophet for adequate vision,
for those days torn from the calendars to rise and reassemble
page by page, have to wait for the oak to climb back into the acorn,

pray until the names for the field wandered back to their source,
the long skein of syllables unwinding through the successions,
Kitfield, Keats Field, Keith's Field, the river reversing its course,

the flame leaping into the matchhead, the oil-soaked wick unlit
again, that set the Huguenot church ablaze, and the hoarse
winds of the hurricane hushed to a held breath in the starlight.

Granted that vision, what might you hope to find here? –
the standing chapel, after the worst wind lashed its spire in 1838
and the steeple passed safe through the storm's eye? But fire

spilled from the lantern where John Keith lay drunk in the vestry,
flames rose despite the rain-swept wind and flooded river,
and all of it – chapel, flame, John Keith – slipped clear of history,

leaving behind a ten-acre tract of dockweed and dried marl,
the still-winged choirs of mockingbirds perched in their hickory
pews, and a story nothing redeems, neither chapel nor pearl.

~

Hard to distinguish memory's embellishments from the prose
of fields, to untangle those prodigal tales wrought at the set table
from the plain-stitched phrasings of bramble and mallow rose.

But, next to Christ's wine at Cana, Noah's dove, and the hot coal
held to the prophet's lips, it all seemed clear enough, that blaze
kindling in my grandmother's talk over purlieu rice and fried quail,

the chapel razed down to charred bricks before the coffee
cooled in her cup and the gravy congealed in its chipped bowl,
so that I knew she had it right, each storm gust and pine tree

fixed in its place, sure as Shadrach's furnace, Nebuchadnezzar,
Eden, or the burning bush. Strange, then, to hear that same story
turned apocryphal in the mouths of uncles and cousins, to hear

the storm winds blown a full month clear of the chapel flames,
the weather so calm that August night not the least leaf or briar
stirred, nor the least bead of rain troubled the window frames,

and those storied bricks, broadcast like fragments of the True Cross
gone, that some claimed lay mortared in a hundred homes,
the church built not from masonwork but heart pine and cypress,

until each detail seemed swept back to that vault of speculation
and possibility where the snowflake is conceived, storehouse
where the hours are forged and kept, where brick and hurricane

alike are kilned or whirled to certainties. What's left but the rage
to believe the past is true, *know* it happened, to believe in blown rain
and chapel ashes, in John Keith who named this fallow acreage

of dockweed when he lay drunk and burning or, sober
as starlight, stuffed the doorjambs and window seams with pages
torn from a dozen bibles, then tossed an oil lamp to light the fire

blazing beyond memory or years?
                          That fire still draws me to the field
where, year after year, neighbors and near relations all swear
It happened yonder, point to where they're sure the lantern spilled,

where those flames still seethe up from the pale roots of sumac
to the first red autumn leaves, and blackberry brambles yield
a fruit sweet as the nectared pulp of sugar cane, growing in black

clusters, big as walnuts, blackberries they swear will boil
down to an ambrosial jam that, kept too long, turns thick
and bitter on the shelf, sharp as a taste of tallow and lamp oil.

The Wife of Job

Well, now, I never heard the whirlwind speak
      to me – though I did lose
my children to a wind storm, saw the lightning's sleek
         flame have its way,
     scorching the servants and the sheep,
      and though I won't deny
that my husband here – the most pious man in Uz –
   still claims an angel whispers in his sleep,
a plain fact that I don't discuss in mixed company.

You've seen such men, eyes dazed with righteousness,
      who think they catch a whiff
of sin in everything: a neighbor's Sunday dress
       hitched just above
    the ankle, or a child's stray smile
     when pies cooled on the stove
or a few idle hours, say, tempt him to mischief.
   Such men may fast, or pray; all the while
salt loses its savor and milk sours in the pail.

And wives grow tired. Oh, not that I complain,
     mind you – but certain nights
Job prayed above me as if Jehovah lay between
      the sheets with us;
    his breath in my hair was like a psalm,
     each spasm a new promise
the heavens might fulfill. Job's ways were just and right,
   no doubting that; though, later, in the calm,
I'd listen to him snore and knew we were alone.

Still, who would strive to be more just than God?
    My husband, I suppose.
And everyone knows that saints are first to feel the rod
     and lash of grace
     descend upon their lives, to bear
      the blade of sacrifice

above their squirming sons, or as the future grows
    in their daughters' wombs, to know they've sown it there –
needless to say, their wives and children share that grace.

    We've sheep and sons to spare now, true enough;
        and I've long salved the sores
that once blistered my husband's skin. But I've no love
        or patience now
    for piety. I do my chores,
        – darn clothes or mend the plow –
and try not to think how such foolishness could stir
    whirlwinds and voices, storms and random fires,
or draw down on us the thunder of the Lord's error.

His Coy Mistress

But at my back I always hear
Time's wingèd chariot hurrying near ...

Spare me the high-flown. Everyone knows that ploy
you tricky swains work up to lift a skirt.
All primped and slicked up, in some thrall of wit,
you fidget, pace around the room a bit
of course, and say, "But Dear, I'll soon be dirt
and you'll be ugly, too, I'd praise your tits
a thousand years if only we had time,
my flat's not far from here, I'm great in bed,
let's eat each other up before we're dead,"
etc., thumb your trousers at the pleats
(vaster than empires, eh? oh clever boy)
and swear that, since it's love, it's not a crime –
the usual hokum. Not that I'm a prude;
and any fool could see beneath the rhyme
to the clear, unsubtle prose of *your* intentions.
But think how the lubricious turns of phrase
and conscience that first prick us on to sex
  – stronger than all the Spanish Fly or X
we slip each other in the chic salons
and parlors, strobe-lit bars and college dorms –
work, in the end, to drop us in the chaps
of time regardless: from bed and back-seat storms
to the old Nuptial Doldrums, the raw paps
and milk-stiff bibs, pramfuls of dozing kids;
from quickies to that painful, tedious wait
at the free clinic for a dose of mercury.
(Valtrex or penicillin if you please).
I'm talking facts here. Oh, we'd have tonight,
there's world and time enough to give our ids
a pleasant stroke, I'm not denying *that*.
But say I felt inclined to take the bait;
we'd spend a few hours in the randy heights,
the rumpled bedsheets of romantic fancy,
both of us hot, hopped up on pheromones

and flatteries, before that wingèd chariot
rolled in with all the sober poignancy
of a busted condom or a ringing phone.
You know the state of things; I could go on.
So, now that the better portion of the night
has packed its moonlit props in and gone home,
before the morning dew lies flushed and plumb
tuckered out where it settles on the lawn,
scrawl your number on a matchbook lid –
I'll ring you later. Time will find us out
in any case, my Dear. And since the sun's
not likely to stand still, I'd better run.

Elegy for Angels

For all the sweet confusion they have caused,
sweeping the air like swallows from the eaves
to strew celestial feathers on the lawn
and spread their rumors of the infinite,
breeding the easy syllables of grace
in strangers' ears, in church or public garden,
for all of their persuasions or the talk
of perfect forms and radiant abstractions,
what good is it to grieve their passing now,
now that their arguments have been diminished
by the sure blaze of autumn's panoply,
the blush of ripe fruit polished on a sleeve?
Most of us here, the faithful to this world,
have long since turned away to other things –
to the certainties of molecule and atom,
extravagance of gold November leaves
which, shaken, reveal to us the mere disorder
of raw sound and the emptied winter branch.

Grown tired of our refusals, how for years
the lavish cadences of mystery
swelling just beyond the garden wall
have continued to elude us, now the angels
have drawn round them their cold robes of starlight
and sulked away to leave us stranded here
among the disenchantments of our longing.
And who among us will remember them
when rivers settle predictably in their courses,
when mustard seeds take root and, blossoming,
flourish uninterpreted in the fields?
So let hours fail into hours, let the lilies
stand as they are, beyond all paradigm;
the angels shall go on singing to themselves,
a whisper in the margins of the visible
that no one hears, that makes the present seem
an elegy for all that follows after.

Noli Me Tangere

Not light itself but what the light reveals:
near the tomb, wild iris and hawthorn,
the wind-combed riggings of spidersilk
strung in the almond leaves.
Violets, too, leaning close to their shadows,
to the light's flaws
that define what is visible.

And what if the spirit were just
this brilliance
revealing the sensual world?

In the garden, for instance, the light
torn like a rib from the infinite
accentuates the grief of the woman's face,
the mouths of lilies opening in the field.

It traces the slender length
of the man's body –
the resurrected Lord, dressed
as a gardener, bearing in his palms
the flaws essential to beauty.

What matters to them
is neither the radiant clarity of sunlight,
nor the seraphim arrayed
in the shimmering gauze of the spirit.

What matters is the mere presence
of the man's risen body,
and the woman
who reaches to touch him but is refused,

who must rely on her faith
in his flesh, that one mystery between them.

The Crux of Martyrdom

Simone Weil at the sanatorium in Ashford, Kent, England. 1943

It's not that she has given up desire
exactly; more like, it seems, the will to choose –
to swallow bread, potatoes, the ripe pear
a nurse has brought her, which she must refuse
for Christ's sake. Or for her people starving in France.
At first she stayed up late, with prayer and cigarettes,
wrote long lies full of tenderness to her parents

> *I have never read the story of the barren fig tree*
> *without trembling. I think it is about me*

telling of friends in London, the spring's rich blossoms;
yet no word about her health, her body's slow
failure. Day after day the doctors come
complaining of her stubbornness. They know
her. And she, their hopes. Still, she must not choose
to eat, must refuse everything save the logic
of refusal, which she cannot help but choose.

> *the most beautiful life possible has always seemed*
> *to me one in which everything is determined*

So her reason revolves along its course
toward that sure consummation for which she waits.
She waits and waits. Too tired now to rehearse
the poem where Love bade His guest to sit and eat,
she dreams of that attic room He led her to,
where bread was sweet, the wine like sun and soil,
and she could see, beyond the attic window,

> *He entered my room and spoke: I understood*
> *that He had been mistaken in coming for me*

a city's wooden scaffoldings, those boats
unladen by a river, and the sun
raging above the trees ...
                    The doctor's coats
Whisper by outside her door. She's alone.
No voice comes down to her; no hallowed word.
Even the headaches have stopped, which once held
her writhing in their vise. And yet she's stirred.

> *when my headaches were raging, I sometimes*
> *had an intense desire to strike someone*

Though it's late, and she's much too tired to write,
she can't quite still the current of ideas
or master her relentless appetite
for thought – philosophy, the worst disease
of a religious mind, perhaps her one
error. For hours she wrestles those abstruse
geometries, turning her whole attention

> *I will consider men's actions and appetites*
> *as though they were lines, surfaces, and volumes*

to the crux of martyrdom. French soldiers
and citizens in thousands have since gone,
quietly or not, to their deaths; how can her
own starvation measure against the ones
who could not choose to choose? Even her days
of factory work – yes, she'd felt the strain
of labor, sweating near the furnaces

> *perhaps He must use even worthless objects*
> *for His purposes: I must tell myself these things*

that scorched her hands and fingers long before
Christ, like a migraine, seized her steady mind;
yet always she could have left. And now the war
has jilted her, denying her the blind
hand of necessity. She's made her choice.
The nurse bends down to take her pulse, offering
a sip of tea; but still she must refuse.

> *if I only had to stretch out my hand to grasp*
> *salvation, I would not put my hand out*

And though she's grown too weak to hold a cup
or spoon, she closes her eyes and sees that room,
that attic room, where she was told to sup,
and the long table shimmers, awaiting Him
who will offer her bread, although she must refuse
until He seat her there among the least
and feed them, too, who have no power to choose –

> *Love bade me welcome: yet my soul drew back*

till the Lord whose bread is hunger sets the feast.

The Oracle's Complaint

There will be time enough for grief, I tell them.
And damn few thank me later for the knowledge.
Right now Oedipus swears by his good fortune,
taking a royal tumble in the nuptial sheets.
Young David's not much trouble *yet* to Saul.
The savior comes to town and heals the blind man,
soldiers get soused and divvy a heap of silver –
there will be time enough for grief; why bother?
Still they come like clockwork, dragging their burdens
and their dull, short-sighted litany of questions,
wanting to know, Will it happen on a Monday?
Was it that time in college with the wall-eyed
majorette? Will she tell her therapist?
As if it matters. No one thanks me later.
Meanwhile the phone lies quiet on its cradle,
and a little sunlight gilds the eaves and awnings,
although the shade beneath is cold, still cold.
The hours wind on their spindle. So I warm up
and toss them a few pearls, the old clichés –
There will be time for trouble later on,
I say; at least for now you've got your health;
the honey in the hive is sweet enough.
Always then some smart ass will point out
bees make their honey with an eye to winter.
But everyone knows just what such winters come to:
the honest desk clerk turns a murderer,
the young stock broker shags the boss's wife.
Some big reversal like a wayward stage prop
comes toppling predictably on their heads.
No one needs an oracle to see that.
And damn few thank me later for the knowledge.
Nevertheless, I give them my advice
before I add the future to their burdens,
though no one listens. Better if they forget
whatever it was that brought them here, the leaf
swiveling from its branch in mild September,

that omen of wind chimes dying on the porch.
(Just think of the Moor cuckolded by his wits:
I saw't not, thought it not, it harmed not me,
and so forth. A dupe, but still he has a point).
For now, I say, why not consider the light
sifting down through the cracked venetian blinds
a promise too ambiguous to guess,
making it past the toss and whirl of motes
to warm you where you sit, brightening
your back, your tea cup on my parlor table?
The boss's wife still kisses him at the door.
The pencil waits unsharpened in its groove.
Soon enough the messengers will come,
the shepherd will tell his story; soon enough
the savior will hang forsaken like the thief.
Don't worry. There will be plenty of time for grief.

Discourse on Desire

By the very right of your senses you enjoy the world.
– Thomas Traherne

I got no apologies for anything I done.
– Donald "Pee Wee" Gaskins

I felt before I thought; for even then I knew my body
was above all else a vessel of virtue, each sense
a means to my salvation – far more than reason,
which often led to error and misfortune. All that my eye
perceived, sleek rondure of flesh, the sun-streaked air
of mountain altitudes, even the least grass blade

> I held the gaff to her throat. The stropped blade
> told her I meant business, and there weren't nobody
> near enough to hear her anyway. It was cold. The sea air
> made her nipples stiffen under the T-shirt, and since
> all night on the road to Myrtle Beach I'd had an eye
> for her sweets, I couldn't see much reason

or stone in the street, was precious beyond reason.
It seemed as if all at once the seraph blade
that barred the estate of innocence was lowered, and I
knew by intuition the ignorant joys of the body,
for even my ignorance was advantageous, every sense
honed for those clear delights to which I was heir,

> to wait. I tightened the belt around her neck; the air
> stopped in her throat, then came slow. She tried to reason
> with me at first, but pretty soon she got the sense
> of things. I twitched her skirt off with my blade,
> then run those cold inches against her bare body
> so she'd know what was coming next. By the look in her eye

and every taste insatiable. No pleasure of the eye
nor appetite in its pure form ever led me to err,
but rather refined the soul to which my body

was wholly wed – for is it not clear by reason
of our very inclinations that the world is ours? No blade
shall sunder man from his bliss if he follow sense.

I'd say she knew. I made her do all that I liked. And since
nothing more was wanted, I looked her in the eye
and told her she'd have to lick the blade
clean before I finished her. She whimpered to the air
that she wouldn't tell. I cut her throat – didn't see no reason
to let her live – and let the marsh crabs have her body.

The eye, needless to say, has its own reasons.
It seeks those various joys to which the sense is heir
when body yields to the blade of appetite.

A Guide to Rousseau

Civilization is somewhat out-of-date
according to the sensitive Jean-Jacques,
who showed young ladies, often to their shock,
a glimpse of Man in his more natural state.

Little Primer of the European Romantic Tradition

1. The Brotherhood of Man, 1793

Robespierre, Pruner of the Royal Tree,
did He who made Rousseau make thee?

2. Nature and the Individual, 1802

Shape nature to your gentle dream, then, Wordsworth,
though not far from those little sylvan hills
where hares are running races in their mirth
the lean fox waits, crouched in your daffodils.

3. The Consolations of Love, 1867

Having watched the girdle of his faith unfurl
along the channel, Arnold in his pain
unfurled the corset of his famous girl
and tupped her five times on a darkling plain.

4. The Brotherhood of Man, 1914

Fine ideals proved little more than trifles.
When the Archduke died, Workers of the World
united, gave up Marx and grabbed their rifles.

Variation on a Theme of Keats

Beauty is truth. That may be true of art.
   As for history, well, it's likely not.
   We've seen the photos. Here's a lovely shot
of sunlit crowds, a heaped potato cart
   on the clean, swept streets of Theresienstadt.

Slow Time

J.M., 1894-1977, small town photographer

Here are fields beyond declension, the wheat
held orient and immortal in our gaze
at just that moment when your shutter stilled
the fixed and failing light –
and all the harvests that time pays
out in these spools of film, in albums filled

with what you meant to keep: a mule and plow
stalled mid-furrow. Leaves stippling the canal.
A Packard engine hoisted from its chassis
and hung from an oak bough,
so far back no one recalls
the date. Yet it strikes us: isn't this history

laid bare – stripped of sequence and consequence,
but no less true for seeming trivial?
The year soldiers charged Normandy and razed
the shell-strafed coast of France,
hawthorn shaded your church steps, kale
leafed out in garden rows, and these bright fields blazed.

꙳

Like history, but on a smaller scale,
you explained years ago to my grandfather.
Now look at this one here: and showed, I'm sure,
a snapshot of Rice Hope plantation, of brambles

snagging the front gate, showed a blackbird caught
mid-flight above Law & Peagler Mercantile –
some moment too idyllic, too pastoral
in its mild charm, removed from the long droughts

and violence, the foreclosures and failed rows
of cotton, corn, and wheat. For five decades
you shelved the Ox Heart chocolates, marmalades,
the cans of pickled turnips and tomatoes

at the Piggly Wiggly, where my grandfather
clerked those years between the responsibilities
of war and family: the past accrues
from such stories of what happened, not from pictures

washed clean of circumstance. And yet we still
cherish the look of things, this place you've made
of barns and back roads, landscapes, light and shade,
and oaks with leaves that, falling, never fall ...

⤳

A slow-minded obsession with what the light
makes of our little time led you here once
to my great-grandfather's feed store, where a sleight
of camera work captured for you the slant

    It happened back when I was a boy – just once
    I remember going down to Daddy's store
    early from school. A black man lay out front,

of sun against the white-washed brick, the grain
and feed sacks in neat rows against the store
window, and that truck, loaded with topsoil,
parked outside by a stunted sycamore

    shot point blank in the face, the bits of brain
    scattered in the gravel. I still remember
    Daddy's chickens pecking at his skull – .

where the Sinclair Oil sign warped in the heat.
Maybe my grandfather drove you out this far
from town one evening after work, eight miles
down Santee Cooper Road, then the paved tar

> Inside the store, my uncle Glennie McKnight
> sat drinking a Cheerwine. This was Prohibition –
> Uncle Glennie'd bring liquor from his stills

U. S. highway that must have gummed the soles
of your boots as you stood there in the late sun
and aimed your lens at the gas pumps and gray
stencil that spelled *R. L.'s Feed.* One by one

> and load it in trucks at Daddy's store. *Hell,*
> Glennie said, *I been meaning to shoot that nigger*
> *for most of a week now – since last Saturday,*

the last fifty years have passed and claimed the scene
piecemeal: so that only five years before
my father was born, those sacks of grain gave way
to auto parts, and just three short years more

> *except I had to keep the kids till Wednesday.*
> *You got a pistol, R. L.? Give it here –*
> *now you take mine*, he said. Then he was gone ...

the store itself was gone, the lot taken over
with thorn apple and vetch. But in your images
that moment survives the progress of the years,
held still in the light, exactly as it was.

᠊

What story's true enough to be believed?
    Not the stalled narrative you've made for us
of sweet gum trees and store fronts, miles of unpaved
    county roads, ripe wheat fields – the detritus
of years, which you took for history. Not yours,
    sylvan historian who couldn't read,
      who lived behind the train depot, alone,
collecting photographs, a makeshift record
    of the place you loved. Now no one here remembers
      seeing you take these pictures of our town.

And even the dead man at that country store
    has failed now into a handful of words
my grandfather said once, words I half-remember,
    half-invent. Sooner or later the words
are all we have, or a few stray images,
    a picture someone took. In the slow light
      of art, you've given us a history
redeemed: bright fields, a Packard engine's weight
    bending a branch. And sun on a feed store's windows
      so beautiful we know it isn't true.

The Music of Farewell

Descending for the last time to the underworld,
the soul of Orpheus addresses the audience.

It's true, of course, that the dusk-umbered leaves
deepening on the hawthorn are a mere sleight
of sun and shadow, true the olive groves
and tamarisks beside the river sway
to an off-key breeze, not to their own delight –
and the blue teal, arrowing through the stray
October clouds, keep to their appointments
according to schedule but not with us in mind,
though you would have it otherwise. What sense
is there in listening to the sun-shot wind
croon through the autumn branches, once the song
behind the song is finished? Always you listened
with your heads tilted toward the absolute
as if the gods would sing to you, while the long
phrase of my sorrow held your world together,
your world of stripped fields and the sweetening fruit
that weights each thick bough earthward. Everywhere
you turned, the lavish music of farewell
lent consequence to things, so that desire
itself became fulfillment to your ear.
And though the mist that swept the cold laurel
was neither Apollo stroking Daphne's hair
nor Ceres weeping at the doors of hell,
though nothing I sang could raise Eurydice
up from the mute depths again, note by note,
it makes no difference now for me to say
the gods are silent, or that the world seems less
for what the hours and seasons claim from us.
More than the sounds that set the stones and trees
in place, and that arrange both shade and light,
a sad music ripens in the heart; caught
between oblivion and paradise,
it enters the world as loss, though in such ways
that the cadences of grief resound as praise.

Gleanings

for Hattie

To see them for what they are, not to make
more of them than the afternoon allows:
starlings among the sweet gum limbs, a rake
propped beneath those leaves the wind will take,
my child gathering feathers beside the house –
a sleight of season, when some moment scatters
its riches across the lawn. Nothing to do
with dates or futures and, I'd guess, small matter
in the year's turning.

                    But I remember, too,
a thousand starlings in my father's yard,
his Chevy in the drive, a smell of leaves
clear as the feather in my daughter's hand –
a swatch of consequence the mind weaves
from history and chance, so that it's hard,
watching it all, not to construe some meaning
from starling, rake, limb, leaf, the child who stands
gathering feathers beneath the shade of wings.

Index of Titles and First Lines

A Note About the Author

Morri Creech was born in Moncks Corner, South Carolina in 1970, and was educated at Winthrop University and McNeese State University. He currently lives in Lake Charles, Louisiana with his daughter Hattie and teaches in the MFA Program at McNeese State University. His poems have appeared in *Poetry*, *The New Criterion*, *The New Republic*, *The Southwest Review*, *The Hudson Review*, *Crazyhorse*, *Critical Quarterly*, *Sewanee Review*, *Southern Review*, and elsewhere. He has published one previous poetry collection, *Paper Cathedrals* (Kent State University Press, 2001), and, in collaboration with the photographer Robert ParkeHarrison, two museum-quality limited editions (*21st*). He has received the Stan and Tom Wick Award from Kent State University Press, a $15,000 Ruth Lilly Fellowship from *Poetry* magazine and the Modern Poetry Foundation, an artist's fellowship from The Louisiana Division of the Arts, and has twice been nominated for a Pushcart Prize.

Other books from Waywiser